HILL 283
CHOP VUM
The Men Behind the Charlie Co. Scarf
in Their Own Words

1615 hrs
Combat
Assault

By P. F. Krause

NEW FORUMS PRESS INC.

Published in the United States of America
by New Forums Press, Inc.1018 S. Lewis St.
Stillwater, OK 74074
www.newforums.com

Copyright © 2020 by New Forums Press, Inc.

Library of Congress Cataloging-in-Publication Data Pending

This book may be ordered in bulk quantities at discount from New Forums Press, Inc., P.O. Box 876, Stillwater, OK 74076 [Federal I.D. No. 73 1123239]. Printed in the United States of America.

ISBN 10: 1-58107-347-X
ISBN 13: 978-1-58107-347-8

Contents

FOREWORD

Charlie Company Veterans recount their experiences of a battle we call "Chop Vum" as documented in this book. This took place on Hill 283 on March 3 - 10, 1969.

These transcripts are in each veteran's own words, making this a very honest, gut-wrenching protrayal of their experiences.

INTERVIEWS
by
KRISTIN HAMILTON
and
PEGGY KRAUSE

We blocked there for three days. We could look off that little hill. We could look out for at least 1,000 meters. There were little groups of twenty, a group of thirty, a group of fifteen. They were marching. They were Communist kind of strutting marching. Give me a break! It's like they were in a break! They were in a garrison area. They were everywhere.

Jamie Hall

We had been mortared before, but they were never on target. But this time, all of a sudden, we heard this screeching sound coming out of the sky --SSSSSSSSS, like sizzling sound - and it was raining mortars on top of us, and they were very much on target this time.

Ernesto Borges

Perez didn't move. He was shaking. The guy next to me said, "Hey! That guys dead." I said "No, he's not. He's not dead." I panicked a little bit, and said to Perez, "No, you're not dead." So, finally I lifted up his head, and his eyes opened wide and shook his head and said he's okay. So, finally I got him moved back.

Rafael Rivera

Then all of a sudden, guys started coming over to help... not a medic, just some other guy. They laid me down in a hole with a couple of the guys in there with me. One guy was hurt real bad and I think his leg was blown off and just faded away and died right there.

Harry Wilmoth

A lot of the time we didn't know what our goal was, we were just told to do this or that and we did it. Sometimes we had no idea what we were doing or why we were doing it, but it was part of survival.

John Stringer

By P. F. Krause / 5

U.S. Army Photograph

I saw Alpha Company and I saw this friend... I saw him and went over and I said, "Thank God you are alright." "You, too," he said, "Since you guys got Captain Hall, you've become a really good company. Everybody talks about what a good officer he is." He really is.

Jay Flannagan

In my headquarters was myself, two radiotelephone operators, and of course, very close to me would be the artillery Forward Observer and his RTO.

Jamie Hall

U.S. Army Photograph

Studying the map before going into the battle at Chop Vum.

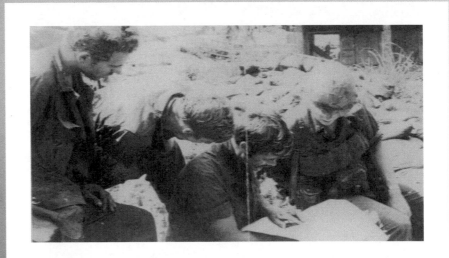

U.S. Army Photograph

After discovering and getting guys in spider holes, an NVA jumped out from behind a tree. He raised his weapon, and as he tried to fire at Charlie Company his weapon jammed. He immediately dropped it and raised his hands in surrender. They tied his hands behind his back and proceeded. When I quesitoned him, he said many, many and gestured with his arms to indicate all around. Vietnamese for many or a lot is rất nhiều. This gave me the indication that we were surrounded.

Jamie Hall

U.S. Army Photograph

Archibald L. J. (Jamie) Hall
"Coyote"

Chop Vum, and any books that I read that refer
to Chop Vum, and any comments I've heard
about Chop Vum, it's been negative.
That is horribly, horribly wrong.
It was not negative if you have the facts. It was a
miracle the thirty-five (Alpha Company) got out.
And it's a miracle that Charlie Company got out.

Captain Archibald L. J. (Jamie) Hall

Nickname: Coyote
Company Commander

The Battle of Chop Vum – As I recall it.

The first time I was introduced to Chop Vum was, as I recall, being in the Operations Center listening to Alpha Company reporting to the Battalion headquarters as to what was going on. They had been inserted into the Chop Vum area, I would assume, just on a Search and Destroy – you couldn't call it that anymore because it is not politically correct – on a reconnaissance trying to find the bad guys. And they did. They would call in reports that concerned me. They would say that they were finding WD1 commo wire, and doing like Fort Benning teaches, they were cutting a large section twelve to fifteen feet out so that it can't be spliced directly. And they had in one case, come back and it had been repaired. That's highly unusual for any NVA organization smaller than a Regiment or a headquarters dug in for a major operation – which they were. I might insert up front here, that there is documentation the 31st NVA Regiment was there and the 33rd was also there to knock off Tam Ky district. There's a military base there also. They had attacked Tien Phouc Special Forces Camp as a diversion. At that time, we thought that was their major effort. Think about that. A special forces camp and all of its outposts along a particular highway were overrun. Tien Phouc was never overrun, but they sure were threatening it.

Back to Alpha company. They also were finding that the equipment the NVA had was brand new. Their pith helmets were brand new and they had a full complement of ammunition for a grenades piece. They had just come down from up North.

The third thing was that Alpha Company was coming across the NVA dug in. They were in a checkerboard pattern. One spider hole in front and the second spider positioned behind it so that it could cover the first one, the third one at an angle where it could cover the second one. The fourth where they could cover the third and the second. I don't recall whether Alpha Company was taking casualties as they discovered these positions. I would assume maybe they were. But again, a very typical NVA defense pattern for one that was more dug in to truly fight.

So, all these things concerned me. I remember talking with the Battalion Commander and giving him my concerns – he was a sharp man. I'm sure he considered it, and we went on with business.

Alpha company, the next thing, calls in and they were being really hammered. They were on a piece of terrain that I would call a sugarloaf. It wasn't a ridge; it wasn't a mountain. It was maybe a fifteen-foot high piece of terrain and it paralleled the river. I don't know the compass direction the river was in. On the other side of the sugarloaf and the river was a long rice paddy running the length of the sugarloaf. Alpha was on one end of this thing, not too far in – they were not far in at all, in fact. I understand there was a stone rice paddy wall running across this sugarloaf. Alpha Company was on one side and the NVA was on the other. Alpha Company was getting hurt pretty bad. Every time they would try to attack, they came under intense machine gun fire and they were taking horrendous casualties. I think we were all there a week or six days for sure. All this time Alpha Company was under fire and really getting hammered. They walked in with 135 and walked out with thirty or thirty-five people. It was next to impossible to get in resupply because of the intensity of the anti-aircraft fire. One Medivac helicopter was shot down. Col. Stinson, the Battalion commander, was killed by .50 Caliber fire trying to kick out ammunition for them.

When I was on top of Chop Vum, I watched a gunship take .50 caliber fire. His turbine was puffing out this vuup, vuup, vuup. Then he'd fly a little bit. Vuup, vuup, vuup. There was just white smoke every time he vuuped. I should say my greatest concern was for the helicopter pilot, but the truth of the matter is I was concerned he was going to crash in my area of operation and they would tell me to go save the helicopter pilot. So, I was quite relieved when I saw him go vuup, vuup, vuup over the horizon.

Now, we were told to be airlifted in and, if you will, save Alpha Company. Go in there and bail them out. So, we went. We went in with 100 people. The first wave that went in – it was a hot LZ, but it wasn't horrendous. Of course, this is all from the perspective of where you are. I'm sure if you were in the first wave it was horrendous. But we didn't take casualties, so it couldn't have been too bad. But it was bad enough. I was on the second wave.

We worked our way in and it's interesting when a company goes into an air assault and you're the company commander. What I had in my headquarters was myself, two radiotelephone operators, and of course, very close to me would be the artillery Forward Observer and his RTO. We were in the center. There were soldiers in front of us – front, left, and front right, and some behind us. We were moving in. Just in my immediate area we had to jump behind a tree and take cover because we were being shot at. My RTO asked for a hand grenade, which I gave him. He threw it into a NVA foxhole, not too far away, and took care of him.

We got up and started to move and a young NVA soldier jumped up from behind some banana plants and pointed an RPD machine gun at us, and it jammed – it didn't fire. For whatever reason – I can't figure out – he didn't get shot. We captured him. He was a seventeen-year-old. Just a kid, and we kept him with us. As we moved forward – it's just so long ago – I don't remember hearing a lot of gunfire, but I'm sure there was.

I do remember that as we moved along, I looked to my left down in sort of like a ravine. Not deep, just some low ground to my left, and there was a field table and a couple of NVA officers standing by this field table. So, that didn't bode well. As we moved forward, I don't remember fire near my group. I can't remember a lot of fire, the grenades and the initial exchange of fire.

It is starting to be sunset. We came to a rice paddy running left and right that we would have to cross. As my memory serves me, across the rice paddy was the beginning of Chop Vum Mountain. A rice paddy running parallel to where Alpha Company was, and up the mountain was where all the bad guys were. It just looked very spooky. We did not want to cross the rice paddy at that time of the evening, much less any other time. So, we stopped. And then to our right, up the mountain, was another rice paddy running. Then at the end of that rice paddy it turned into vegetation and it got a little steeper and there was a draw that went up the mountain. At the base of that was a farmer's hooch that I couldn't see at that time. To the right of that was an open area.

I told first platoon leader, Raul Alvarado, who was behind me… I think I had gone to the front to look at the rice paddy crossing. I told Raul to go on up there and secure a perimeter for the night. He began to go up the hill and they came under fire. Raul was killed and three other men were killed. I think one was a brand-new sergeant who was only in country a couple of weeks. So, they were killed, and it was starting to get dark, so we pulled our horns in. We were not in the best posture in the world – being pretty much three platoons strung out in a column. Not single file column – but first platoon, second platoon, and third platoon kind of bunched up. I'm sure we went into defensive posture down there. That night we didn't have any problems at all. One man was brought to my command post – I forget his name – but he died the next morning or during the night.

The next morning, we went up the mountain – the same direction I told Raul to go. But this time the men from the first platoon went to the left and flanked that wall. My understanding is that they killed a few NVA behind that wall. I also remember that they saw some spider holes there. I don't know… in the situation we were in I'm a little suspicious of spider holes, but they could have been there.

Then we moved up – this is a little confusing for me. I believe we moved up the side of the mountain and we dug in up there. At the time we were up there we saw a medivac helicopter down across that rice paddy going up Chop Vum where the farmer's house was. And, low and behold, a CH47 Blacksmith came and landed and started to rig the helicopter to take it up. I couldn't believe it. We couldn't get helicopters in to get our dead and wounded out or this little Vietnamese prisoner out. Anybody that flew around us was getting shot down. Col. Stinson, the Battalion Commander, was kicking ammunition out to help Alpha Company and he was shot and killed. The gunship was shot. I don't know how they did it. I don't know how anybody in their right mind sent them out to get it.

But anyhow, we saw NVA trying to sneak on them. Because of our higher elevation, I would assume we shot at them, because the blacksmith took off with the helicopter. Amazing.

At some point in time, ammunition was kicked out at us from the rice paddy where we did not want to cross. I wasn't real certain I wanted to go out there even to get ammunition. We wanted to get a wounded man out of there. When that helicopter landed there was sniper gunfire and some major that was delivering the ammunition for us was shot sideways through the bridge of his nose. That's close. They had to take off, so they just kicked the ammunition out. They didn't have time to take the wounded man on board. They had to get out of there or there was going to be another helicopter sitting in the rice paddy with dead people. So, they took off and the wounded man and everybody came back. We were confounded … what are we going to do?

We spent the night again. The next morning the NVA had probably gotten to the farmers and that rice paddy was flooded with about a foot of water. To make a long story short – we were trying to figure out how were we going to get the ammunition because we needed it.

Bravo Company, Captain Brian Chenault, showed up. I'm not sure exactly where he was at the time, but he showed up. He gathered up some village people and he told them, "Go get it!" It was mostly women, four or five of them, screaming and wailing. But they went out there and they got all the ammunition and brought it back to the jungle. The NVA didn't shoot any of them. So, we got ammo resupply.

The next day we got a helicopter to come in that picked up the KIA and the Vietnamese prisoner. They were evacuated.

I'm not sure whether it was that same day or the next day that we proceeded up the mountain. It might have been the same day because we didn't go that terribly far when sunset came up. But then again, it was raining – drizzling. It was black as could be and you couldn't see… so it could have been the next day. I don't know.

An interesting segway is that I spoke North Vietnamese. I talked to this little seventeen-year-old NVA soldier and he told me, essentially, that we had attacked the rear of his company. His company was part of the battalion that was protecting regimental headquarters. If you think of a bow and arrow target where regimental headquarters was the red bullseye, we LZ'd in the next ring which was behind their defense. Their defense was looking outward. They were very confused. The thing that disturbed me was that nobody at Division, nobody at Brigade must have talked to this kid. This kid told me there was a battalion in defense of a regiment. At that time, Tien Phouc is being attacked. At least a battalion or two battalions are involved in that. So, here's an NVA regimen and we're in the middle of it. This kid tells us that. Nobody seems to realize it. If anything, they're saying, "You gotta move faster." Well, anytime you moved fifty yards you ran into the NVA. They were everywhere. Later I learned that it was the 31st Regiment, which is in official books. I'm not sure if the 33rd NVA Regiment is now in the official books or not, but they were there, too. That was confirmed by a personal friend of mine. He was a lieutenant, MI, who was responsible for tracking and maintaining contact with the 33rd NVA. He said he lost them moving south in the area of Chop Vum when this battle happened. There were a lot of them. To me that means there were 6,000. Maybe 8,000 NVA staging to knock off Tam Ky district, and the Special Forces Camp was just a diversion. Think about that – the Special Forces Camp being a diversion. In the months preceding that there was nothing, really, in the American Division that equaled the Special Forces Camp getting hit. We had firebases hit. I don't think we had any overrun, but they were close. But a Special Forces Camp? No. So that was a big deal. But nobody listened.

That night that we're up behind Chop Vum, you could look down. So, we weren't in the jungle. We were in a meadow. A long meadow bordered by the jungle going down the mountain. Chop Vum could have continued to go much higher, and this was just sort of a meadowy breakdown below, because it's a big mountain and its jungle. Because where we were up the jungley mountain, there was an open area. I bet the mountain continued upward. I know it did because we were farther down. I could see across the rice paddy and I could see black uniform guys, three of them, trying to run around the wall and hunker down looking to see if they could shoot at Alpha Company people behind that wall.

We stopped that night and we had pretty good perimeter because of that open area. It became rainy, misty. No moon. Very dark. You couldn't see your hand if you waved it in front of your face. I think a day earlier, Major Neary, I forget his first name – a WestPoint guy and just a sterling character – came down there to be present on the ground. Neary and I couldn't figure it out because he needed to be back at Battalion.

The Battalion Executive Officer had four days until he went home, and he refused to go to the field. The Battalion Commander had been killed. So that left Major Neary of the three. Instead of leaving him at battalion – a man that knows the battalion, that knows these companies and has worked with them, a man to take command and run it from the operations center – they send him out to the field with me. He can't see any farther than I can. It made no sense.

That night it was pitch black. It was dark – you couldn't see. We could hear the NVA digging in not too far from us. That said, about the time it was so dark you couldn't see, Major Neary got a call on his radio from Brigade, "We want you to move tonight down to blocking a position." The blocking position was at least a kilometer, maybe a little bit farther. To get to it we would have had to go through a jungle. We would have had to leave the meadow area and turn to the left and drop down to the jungle. You couldn't see your hand and I did not want to take casualties.

Here we could hear their trenching tools digging in – metallic noises. We were ordered to move 1200 meters down to a blocking position. We'd have to cut back into the jungle, and through the jungle essentially to where they were. I was not willing to take casualties and not be able to medivac them. So, I also wanted to get the opinion of a Chieu Hoi who was one of very few Chieu Hoi's that I thought was excellent. I'm glad he left the VC or NVA because he was very good. The fact that he wasn't with them anymore was a benefit to us. I called him and I asked him what the situation was, and what his opinion was. He said, "Captain, tonight we're going to die." I thought, "OK, that's interesting input." So, I told Major Neary, "I'm not going to move because I don't want to take casualties and not be able to get them out." Major Neary, to his credit, said "I'm the senior officer on the ground. I will say that it is my decision." And he did. Because of all this Chop Vum stuff he broke out in hives. They had to take medical care of him, and that's when he had to leave.

So, we didn't go. The Brigade Commander was so furious that he wanted to come out and relieve Major Neary. I don't know if the Brigade Commander wanted to take command or what. Now it was so rainy and monsoony and ugly – this is what I've been told from people who were on the Brigade staff – the helicopter pilot was flying and he said, "Colonel, I'm not flying in this, we've got to turn back." Colonel Tully got pretty indignant and the pilot said, "I don't care. We are going back." So, they returned. The Brigade Commander was pretty upset about that.

The next day at daylight we got up and went down to the blocking position. In route to the blocking position, from my perspective in my position in the company column, there was sniping going on. I heard people say people were hit. I don't remember people being hit, because we didn't medivac anybody out. We didn't carry any wounded. We didn't have supply, medivac, or anything until later on in blocking position when we were mortared, and they brought in Medivac helicopters.

Up until then there were no helicopters and we didn't carry wounded. We were sniped at. I know we were crossing this little roping area and you stagger it. You don't go one, two, three, four. We were running across. I remember when I ran across. "CRACK!" But fortunately, they were a lousy shot – nobody was hit. So there was a little bit of sniping going on. I thought, "That ain't good."

We got down to the edge of this rice paddy. It was a very narrow rice paddy. It ran down from the river and away from the river. Across this little narrow rice paddy was this tiny little ridge – not a ridge, really – more like a sugarloaf. And on one edge of it toward the river was a 750 lb. bomb crater. We had to cross that rice paddy. We could see the NVA walking around on this ridge. I thought this would be a hot attack across the ridge, but we're going to have to go over there. Some of the men said, "Sir, they're behind us." I don't know if they were sniping at us, but I just was under the impression that they were behind us. I thought, "Let's get some smoke going." Artillery smoke.

This is a personal deal. I was sitting on the edge of the jungle. Across from me was the FO and his RTO. On my side was me and my three guys – secure and two RTOs. One of the smoke rounds ejected the smoke canister and this 105-steel canister tumbling through the sky hit the ground between the group. It didn't hit anybody. It just went "whack! Brrrrrr." We were all so busy. We were so busy that it was not a big deal.

Pete Beascachia, one of the best FOs in the world – a Dominican – of course, cancelled the artillery. I passed the word up and down to put the bayonets on, but come to find out, I don't think 50% of the guys had bayonets.

I had one platoon, I think it was the third platoon, and their most senior person there was a Specialist 4th class or maybe an E5. His nickname was Muff Walls. Jerry Walls. He came up with the platoon leaders and he said he didn't want to be responsible. I'm thinking, "I don't need this right now." I said, "Ok. That's good. But if we don't do this, we're going to DEROS right here.

How about your buddy?" I forget his buddy's name – we'll say Smith. "How about if you and Smith both do it?" ... "OK."

Thank goodness, he and Smith were the platoon leaders of seventeen men or twenty, if there were that many. We attacked across the rice paddy. Where I was, we didn't receive any fire, and if we did, I didn't hear it. You got to realize that at that time there is so much going on. There could be a little bit of fire and it doesn't register because it's not a lot.

We got up on this ridge. At a Charlie Company reunion Jerry Collins told me, "No. I shot an officer way down on the right. I got his pistol. Everybody was jousting for my pistol."

Then over here, everybody was saying, "I shot a guy over here." We were shooting them over here and over there. So, there were NVA there and the guys were shooting them. But there were no NVA foxholes there. Interesting. So, what were they doing just walking around up there? Who knows? There were 8,000 of them. They were everywhere. They might have been having a picnic up there.

Anyway, we got up there and there was an ancient rice paddy wall running on the jungle side where we attacked across. The rice paddy wall ran left to right and it was just down off the crest. The people on that side kind of dug in and got behind that. Jerry Collins was behind that and he sniped and killed a few people. They didn't know where we were. There was a jungle trail that paralleled that little rice paddy. They walked along and they didn't know we were there. They'd just be ho hum walking along that trail, and he'd shoot one. He shot one guy that had a machine gun and he must have been the meanest machine gun sergeant in the world because he sent another guy to retrieve the machine gun and Jerry shot him. I think they got the machine gun when it got to be nighttime.

One guy was trying to sneak away and was hiding behind some botanica banana leaves. Of course, they were short people. He thought he was camouflaged. Someone shot him. He dropped the banana leaves and just crumpled upon the ground.

They were everywhere. Confused. They knew where Alpha was. After we got on the hill in this "blocking position" which may have been blocking the NVA. But, the NVA were already thick right across the mountain. I don't think our blocking there was denying NVA access to Alpha Company. There were other avenues of approach. But on a map from Brigade, I'll give them credit. We got them blocked.

Here's the problem. We blocked there for three days. We could look off that little hill. We could look out for at least 1,000 meters. There were little groups of twenty, a group of thirty, a group of fifteen. They were marching. They were Communist kind of strutting marching. Give me a break! It's like they were in a garrison area. They were everywhere. So for people that are critical of this fight you have to move fast; you gotta do this and do that. They got to wake up and realize that you have a company of 100 men in the midst of 8,000 NVA. You need to consider that. For what was there and what happened, Charlie Company did a brilliant, magnificent job. The good Lord lead us out of there because when it was all over nothing could be done.

They tried dropping tear gas, eight-inch artillery fire and nothing would get the NVA to back off of Charlie Company. I called in aircraft and they hosed the area. The aircraft dropped napalm and bombs because I knew the FAC [Forward Air Controller]. I guess in a crisis they will do it, but they do not like to drop perpendicular to the line of troops. They'll drop parallel, but they don't want to drop perpendicular because the 250-pound hydriodic bombs, every once in a while, the fins pop out and one of them will blow off. That bomb tumbles, and it falls short, and it goes off. But Jack the FAC, a good friend of mine, who piled into the ground supporting the 101st Airborne Division up north later on. He had airplanes stacked up in the sky. Because I made friends with him at Brigade before coming in the field, every morning before he would fly somewhere on assignment, he would get on my company frequency and he said, "Do you need any help?" Woa! What an asset!

So, he brought them in, and we smoked them on the bottom of Chop Vum. He said there were secondaries all over that looked like popcorn. My understanding is later on when they went in to retrieve Bravo Company's dead, they discovered 350 dead NVA. I would assume that most of that was bombed.

Anyhow, we were on this blocking position for three days. All of a sudden Brigade says, "You got to attack." We were to go up on that sugarloaf area and relieve Alpha Company. I didn't want to. I told Major Neary, "We've been sitting here and we can see all these clowns marching 1,000 meters away. They can see us walking around. They know we're here. They're waiting for us to do something. If we do, they're going to smoke us with mortars. He told me, "I refused a command a couple of nights ago. I can't do it again."

I told him, "Ok, but we're going to take casualties."

He said, "We gotta do it." I said, "Yes, sir. Let's go."

And we did. We launched our attack and we immediately came under mortar fire. I took the most casualties that I had taken in six months in Charlie Company. Just in that one moment. But, I guess we had to do what we had to do.

There was a bomb crater. Some people went in the bomb crater. Unfortunately, a mortar round went in there and killed and wounded people. My RTO was killed. My second RTO had his kidney punctured with shrapnel. I was headed for that hole, but Pete Beascachia, the FO, grabbed my leg as I was running by and said, "Coyote! Get In here! Get down! Quick, get in here!" So, I just plopped down there. He and his RTO were in his foxhole and there wasn't any room for me. Mortars were going off all around. This is personal again, but if I'd have gone in there I'd have been severely wounded or D-E-A-D. But, you know what? Every day was like that. That was the battle of Chop Vum.

They told us, "You're gonna have to fight your way out. There's nothing else we can do."

Here's another side note: Brigade, Division did not have reinforcements. No reinforcements. We were out there on our own. They said, "It's all we can do."

Now Alpha Company was down to thirty-five people. Now think about this: These thirty-five guys were probably throwing up so often and going absolutely nuts waiting for… them to get killed. Terrified. All of a sudden, they get told, "You got to fight your way out." They're sayin', "Hell, we've been trying to fight our way out for five or six days."

They tell me, "You got to fight your way out." I knew what was around there. What we had just come through and I thought, "Ya. We are going to fight our way out."

We started marching up. Praise the Lord – not a shot fired. And that's Alpha Company, also. When we walked out, Alpha walked out. When we got picked up, I think in a grassy area – probably not too far that night – we didn't move.

I think Alpha Company got moved up to the rice paddy where they were. Not one shot fired!

The best thing I can think of is the United States Air Force smoked them so bad. It was a perfect bomb run. Running parallel down the enemy's position. Just perfect. And all those secondary missiles? I think they just said, "It just ain't worth it. It ain't worth it." And they aborted their mission to attack Tam Ky. They never attacked Tam Ky.

I think the Special Forces attack was going according to plan. I think Alpha Company stumbled right in the middle of them. They decided to wipe out Alpha Company. Then they sent me in. I can't recall for sure if Bravo Company went out, but I guess they did because they helped with the ammo.

I think they thought, "OK, the jigs up. These Americans – they're going to pile on us, and we're going to suffer too many casualties and not accomplish our mission." So, Hanoi said, "Boogie!"

So, I think the only thing it could have been was the bombing. Alpha company wasn't hurting them. We were not significantly hurting them. It had to be the bombs.

Chop Vum, and any books that I read that refer to Chop Vum, and any comments I've heard about Chop Vum, it's been negative. That is horribly, horribly wrong. It was not negative if you have the facts. It was a miracle the thirty-five (Alpha Company) got out. And it's a miracle that Charlie Company got out.

Amen.

Additional Comments:

After discovering and getting guys in spider holes, an NVA jumped out from behind a tree. He raised his weapon, and as he tried to fire at Charlie Company his weapon jammed. (I was already in front.) He immediately dropped it and raised his hands in surrender. They tied his hands behind his back and proceeded. When I questioned him, he said many, many, many and gestured with his arms to indicate all around. Vietnamese for many or a lot is *rất nhiều*. This gave me the indication that we were surrounded.

Ernesto Borges
"Borges"

Then a mortar round hit behind me. People were screaming, "Medic! Medic! Medic!" some were calling for themselves. Some were calling for other people.
Harry was calling because Dean Veale had been hit, and he was calling for him.
People were screaming.
A round went off behind me. I got hit. Blood started rushing down my arm. I was hit in the shoulder…

Ernesto Borges
Mortar Platoon

They called me Borges.
Nobody knew my first name, which is Ernesto.

I did not know name of the place we were going. I was a Spec. 4, so I wasn't privy to a lot of information. They just tell you were going to a CA (Combat Assault) and we knew it was a pretty hot area. We always start out on the helipad waiting for the helicopters to come pick us up.

I always had a habit of walking up and down looking at the guys, because typically somebody wasn't going to come back. Either someone was going to get killed, or someone was going to get wounded – whatever reason. And I used to try to look into their eyes and look for some sign wondering if it was me or if I was going to be the one, but you could never tell.

Anyway, I remember the helicopters coming and we were taken to that area. I had no idea where we were. We were jumping off the helicopter from maybe six, seven, eight feet above the ground from the choppers into the rice paddies. The choppers couldn't let you down, they dropped you down to get away quick as possible, too, so you were just airborne jumping off the choppers into the rice paddies.

I can't recall exactly what happened each day, but I know that each day as we went through the jungle, to the best of my recollection, the point man was killed pretty much on a daily basis.

I remember walking. Me and Alvarado. We just played poker a couple of nights before. And I remember looking down and seeing he'd been shot. Mortally wounded.

I don't know many of the other guys. At that time, I had been put into the weapons platoon, (I had been transferred), therefore, I didn't have to walk point anymore. That was a blessing that probably saved my life, because I knew that I would have been walking point. My number would have come up. You alternated platoons, you alternated squads within the platoon, and alternated individual soldiers, but my number always came up when I was in the other Platoon. But when you're in the mortar's platoon you don't have to walk point, so it wasn't my responsibility.

I remember someone whose turn it was to walk point and he refused. He threw his weapon down, they took his weapon and he walked through the jungle without a weapon during that mission. He just wouldn't do it. Later I talked to him and he said, "I wanted to live, and I just wasn't going to do it." That's something I wouldn't have done, but sometimes people can't take pressure. You look and see four days in a row all the point guys killed and it's your turn and you say, "What are the odds?" He's probably a grandfather somewhere now. So, somebody had to take his place, of course.

It was a rough mission, and it culminated for me the day we had the mortar attack. It was March 8, 1969. And my recollection was that we were set up in a very open area. I said to a guy by the name of Thomas Gregson, "Gregson, why don't you talk to the CO. Maybe we should spend the night somewhere else and not here."

Gregson was the RTO (Radio Telephone Operator). He said, "Let me go talk to the Captain." And he walked away from me and standing with me was Doc Brown, who was our medic – I think Doc Himan was one also. And Gregson walked away, and we were talking, and I said, "I'm going to dig in deeper." Those were my exact words. "I don't like digging foxholes, but I think tonight, I'm digging foxholes, because it looks like it's dangerous here."

Shortly thereafter, we heard these sounds which we knew to be mortar rounds being discharged. And it's a very distinctive sound – thoop, thoop, thoop, thoop. The mortars are being dropped into tubes and they come out and come down. We had been mortared before, but they were never on target. But this time, all of a sudden, we heard this screeching sound coming out of the sky – SSSSSSSSS, like sizzling sound – and it was raining mortars on top of us, and they were very much on target this time. When you hear the sound, you can't tell where the round is going to land – on top of you, next to you, fifty yards away. Going through your mind I remember just getting down to the ground. That is what you are taught – take a low position. I remember my face was to the ground. Just to tell you the story (it's kind of weird): I remember looking down and seeing an ant and the ant was going down into the hole and I wished I were that ant and could have gone into that hole. I remember that so vividly how lucky that insect was to be able to go down into that hole.

I remember looking down, I was in a higher position than some, and rounds started dropping. One hit right in front of Jay Flanagan, just a few feet in front of his head. He was in a prone position. And I saw the back top of his helmet and I didn't know how severely injured he was.

Then a mortar round hit behind me. People were screaming, "Medic! Medic! Medic!" some were calling for themselves. Some were calling for other people. Harry was calling because Dean Veale had been hit, and he was calling for him. People were screaming. A round went off behind me. I got hit. Blood started rushing down my arm. I was hit in the shoulder. When a round hits shrapnel just spreads.

So, I made a decision at that time. I said, "I can lie here or try to do something." I just had to do something, so I jumped up and I ran to the highest point I could find, and I just started firing in the direction the mortars were coming from. I looked and saw Captain Hall; he was lower on the hilltop. He looked up at me and he grabbed his weapon and he came up and joined me and the two of us laid out a lot of lead. The mortaring stopped. Then I looked around to see people hurt, people screaming. There was a big B52 crater and on the top of the crater was a guy by the name of Ken Miller, who had actually been a bunker-mate at one time, and he was dead. I went to him first. Part of his torso and his buttock was severely severed, and he was dead.

And I went further down the crater and there was Thomas Gregson. I was the first one to get to Gregson. He just left me two minutes before. He was covered with sand, like beach sand, and it was mixed with blood. His insides were outside, and his leg was gone, and his bones were exposed. The first think I thought of was: Boy, is his fiancé still going to want to marry him? He had maybe thirty days or less. He was a short timer. And he was getting married in October. "When I get home, and I'm going your wedding, and so on. We had talked about that and his fiancé. A lot of us had got "Dear John" letters – I had gotten one, Veale had gotten one, a lot of guys had gotten "Dear John" letters. But here's a guy whose girlfriend, fiancé, was still waiting on him. Of course, it was a great thing, I was happy for him. Now how was she going to feel with him having only one leg? Then I realized that he wasn't going to survive. That was nothing that you could patch up. Nothing I could do. I could try to find a medic. Maybe he could do something, pull out some magic, but I doubt it.

There was another guy, Frank Rae who was right below him. Frank was hit in the back leg, buttocks area. I went to get a medic; I went to find Doc Himan. He was a very good friend of Tom Gregson. I told Doc what happened, and he was totally distraught. Gregson was probably his best friend in the company because they had gotten mononucleosis at the same time and spent a couple of the weeks in the hospital together and had become very close.

I actually had to hold Doc Himan down to the ground for a few seconds until he composed himself because he took it pretty badly. Then I took him over to Gregson. There wasn't a lot that could be done. We took Gregson over to a different area along with the other guys. The choppers came in and the people who were most severely wounded were put on the first choppers. The people who were not ambulatory were put on those choppers.

Then it was like a triage. The walking wounded, the least severely wounded, and the dead. So, leaving, I was on the last chopper out with Gregson, Veale, and Miller. I remember the three of them were piled up right in front of me. I was on the left-hand side of the copper. John Stringer was on the chopper, also. He was on the right-hand side. There were a couple of guys in the middle. I remember the chopper took us to the hospital. It was like something out of a movie. We landed and hospital personnel came with wheelchairs and gurneys. And a couple of guys were taken in wheelchairs. Stringer was some of them. He went in first. I was the last guy off of the chopper, other than the pilot.

It seemed like an interminable walk from the chopper into the "hospital" – for lack of a better term. And when I got in that room there were guys; Stringer was in there, and Smokeburner (there was a guy we called Smokeburner). Smokeburner's lungs had been punctured with shrapnel. I can recall the doctors and nurses taking some kind of device and water would shoot out of it. They had a saline solution and I remember some of the guys screaming in agony – not so much the room, but the probe going in and shooting the saline water in there. And then I went to another room. The doctor said, "Get on your stomach," and he took a scalpel and cut a crater in my right shoulder to take the shrapnel out.

I can't recall what happened, but later than night (I was not hospitalized as many people were, I went back to the rear and was assigned a bunker) the first sergeant... (we called him "Top," but I don't remember his name) but, Top came in and Red drove the jeep (Red was assigned to the rear earlier). Red was driving the jeep. Top said, "I need you to go with me to identify the bodies." I remember the ride we took to the morgue. Because I was there and had not been hospitalized, and I knew those guys, I had to identify all three of the bodies.

Jay Flanagan

I remember that I got stuff under my fingernails – it sticks up in the quick (of the nail).
There was dust and smoke all around me.
I turned around and pulled out and there's Ernie Borges – he said, "You are alive, I thought you were dead!" I said, "So did I. Boy, am I happy to see your face."
I knew I wouldn't see him in Heaven, so I knew I must be alive.

Jay Flannigan
Mortar Platoon

Before we went out, we had word that Alpha Company was out there and in a world of hurt, which was very interesting to me because a fellow I had gone through training with was in Alpha Company. So, I wondered about him.

And then we were sent out, and as we heard, it was a hot LZ and the guys were getting shot at right away. The point man got shot as he went over a berm, or a rise in the path. One of the other fellows went to get him and he got shot, then Lt. Alvarez. I think he was the third one to try to get to those two, and he go shot, and another one. We were in the back because we were in the weapons platoon. But they got a guy to stop and pull back to and they were able to get them out. We called in artillery on the position that he was firing from – he or they.

At some skirmishes there were a lot of wounded and they couldn't come in and get them out. If I do remember right, some of the guys we were carrying around died of shock because they weren't able to get out, from loss of blood. Really, a bit despairing. How are we going to get these guys out if we're having so much trouble? We finally called in the jets to bomb the area ahead of us. After the jets stopped, Bruce Adams – he's from Minnesota – he came up to me and pulled up his shirt and had some shrapnel from the jet in his back.

Our job, as I understand it, was to push back and go up the hill so that Alpha and Bravo Company could come in behind us. They would come the next day with the helicopters and get everyone.

As we went up on the hill we heard the "thunk," which was the mortar. And being in the motor platoon, I could tell it was coming our way. There was a bomb crater off to my right and I ran towards it and I could tell that the mortar was going to hit before I got there, so I hit the ground just before I got to the bomb crater and the mortar went in the bomb crater, I believe. I think that is where John Stringer, Harry, and Dean all got injured.

I remember that I got stuff under my fingernails – it sticks up in the quick (of the nail). There was dust and smoke all around me. I turned around and pulled out and there's Ernie Borges – he said, "You are alive, I thought you were dead!" I said, "So did I. Boy, am I happy to see your face." I knew I wouldn't see him in Heaven, so I knew I must be alive.

Then we got everybody together as best we could, with the injured, and helped them down the hill.

Another fellow, Cooney – he was from Arizona – he came from another platoon, and he got shrapnel in his neck. I patched him up and I said, "Let's go." Then he dropped his pants and he had all kinds of shrapnel in his butt. I said, "Cooney, why me?" so I patched him up and brought him down.

One of the hardest moments was a fellow from Staten Island – his name was Sal – came to the Company not long before this. I said, "You're lucky to come to the Mortar Platoon, because in the Mortar Platoon nobody's been killed. Now we got Dean killed. He came to me and said, "Nobody gets killed, huh?" I felt really bad – like I lied to him. But, I didn't. It just doesn't always work out like you hope. And when we got down to the bottom, now all of a sudden the rockets are coming at us. It was like they were coming in slow motion. Right towards me – and I hopped into an old foxhole. And as I'm hopping in, it seemed up on the hill they honed in on the old foxholes and bomb craters because they figure that is where the guys are going to go. That's where we got some damage with a few rounds before Borges started firing at them. Then Captain Hall and I and some other guy did and they took off.

But the rocket went past us and hit the side of the hill and hit behind us and not near anybody. And I believe, I'm not sure, but I believe that was the fellow who was covering him[self] with the banana leaf and Jerry Colins took him down with some shots with his long-range site.

Then it started getting dark. The other companies were coming in behind us so we needed to go all the way back so they had room. Then in the morning they bring us all up on this clearing surrounded by trees to give the helicopter some cover. I saw Alpha Company and I saw this friend – darned if I can remember his name – I saw him and went over and I said, "Thank God you are alright." "You, too," he said, "Since you guys got Captain Hall, you've become a really good company. Everybody talks about what a good officer he is." He really is.

Then the helicopters came in. I remember one getting hit and going down – one of the gunships. Vince Tabor didn't want us to leave. He wanted us to go find him. I believe they wanted Alpha Company first because they were the hardest hit and they wanted to get those guys, and we went out last and got out pretty much without incident.

Harry Wilmoth

I raised my head up and got hit in the back of my neck. It felt like someone hit me with a baseball bat. I reached up and grabbed it and my finger went in the hole and I passed out. When I woke up, I had blood all over everything.

Harry Wilmoth
Mortar Platoon

Before we went in, Captain Hall got a 90 recoilless and came to weapons platoon to see if anyone wanted to carry it. I said I'll take it…it was 90 mil (four inch diameter) about four feet long, weighing about forty pounds. It looked like a bazooka. It shoots a projectile out the front and blows an explosion out back. We had Armor Piercing Rounds about ten pounds…nails about an inch long with a little arrow on the end and it would just scatter out. Anti-personnel rounds about eight pounds. High explosives eleven pounds… The sight had three scales depending on what round you chose. We spent three to four days practicing on the LZ with the sights and rounds. Stringer and I worked with it and I got tuned in to where I could get a feel for it. It was so different than anything we had used or seen.

So, I carried the recoilless, a .45 handgun, and three or four rounds. And John had four rounds and maybe some other people carried some, I don't remember. (You had to wear ear plugs…if you didn't, you couldn't hear anything for about fifteen minutes.) If I remember correctly, we were just sitting on the skids with the recoilless. It was a hot zone and we were five to six feet above the water and Stringer and I and some others jumped out and when we jumped out, we jumped feet first. When I jumped in, I was in the mud up to my chest and the guns were firing at us from the jungle and the waters started jumping everywhere from the bullets. John was able to get out to the jungle and I had a four foot piece of pipe on my shoulder and I was stuck.

I just got in the jungle and couldn't move…and then a grenade dropped in right by us. The sergeant that was with us grabbed it and it didn't go off…it was a dud. We started to push and push and push and finally some of the guys went up and down just a bit and I believe that's when Raul Alvardo got killed. And I think a few others were killed and some guys were pinned down. So when we were able to link up with everyone there was a machine gun in the jungle and we didn't know where, so they had us come up …

There were some banana trees there and we crawled up by the trees and we put an anti-personnel round in and I did the best I could and fired and it was about seventy feet and everything just fell, it opened it right up… but in the explosion of the recoilless the banana trees fell down and we were in the open. So, we pulled the breech open and loaded it up again and just then the machine gun opened up on us again; but when he shot, I knew exactly where to shoot. He shot first and missed. We shot second and got him. We got the bodies and the wounded back.

I believe the next time we fired, there was a rock wall we were taking fire from and we had good direction of where they were. John and I put an Armor Piercing round in and blew them away.

The Armor Piercing Rounds…when they hit, they had an eight inch shaft sticking out and the shaft would hit and it would have another explosive charge behind it. It would blow thru whatever it hit. It was so powerful it could go thru three to four inches of steel. It just blew the wall to smithereens and shrapnel all over.

Then the next time we fired it was at least the next day and they were trying to get choppers in to get supplies in to us. The jungle had a trail and it kind of came along and went straight to the rice patty and the other side was a hill and a tree or stump or something. So anyway, Col. Stinson ordered his chopper to pick up the ammo we needed and at that time I was designated to carry Ranger's body. He (the other guy) was in front and I was in back (I had the shoulders). Col. Stinson's chopper came down and he was throwing supplies out and we were trying to throw the bodies in and all of a sudden they (NVA) opened fire on us and Stinson got shot and fell down in the chopper…then the chopper took off. I knew Stinson was shot bad. Then the other guy got shot in the shin (I don't remember his name). I got him back to the jungle, the medic came up to take care of him and sent Stringer with the recoilless and loaded an Armor Piercing round and blew him away. The good thing was I knew exactly where the guy who was shooting at us was...

We took the gun and withdrew. Other people got the supplies and the stuff that Stinson threw out. Later that day they were able to get the bodies out and supplies in … all we got was ammo. I ditched the .45 handgun and got an M16 so I had some protection.

Every night we pulled position, and everyone was up and you could hear things going on … it all runs together. I believe it was the next day, that's when we moved onto an open area and the NVA was shooting mortars at us. When the first round started coming in, I hit the ground — you could hear them before they hit. The first round hit Monger, he got hit in the chest. I raised my head up and got hit in the back of my neck. It felt like someone hit me with a baseball bat. I reached up and grabbed it and my finger went in the hole and I passed out. When I woke up, I had blood all over everything. I reached up and touched the hole. Monger was gasping and bleeding and I had him lean to one side and told him I'd try to get a medic. That's when I saw Dean Veale on the ground ten to fifteen feet from me. His left butt was blown off; you could see the hip joint and the tendons going over the joint ... no flesh, just exposed.

When I saw him (Veale), he had holes all up and down his left side. His right leg was trying to push and his right arm was trying to crawl ... so I really had to try and find a medic. Stringer was hit, too, and I don't remember.

Then all of a sudden, guys started coming over to help … not a medic, just some other guy. They laid me down in a hole with a couple of the guys in there with me. One guy was hurt real bad and I think his leg was blown off and just faded away and died right there. Another guy had been shot thru the kidney.

I don't know how long we were there but then we were loaded on a chopper … and I tried to walk around and was just seeing spots in my eyes and getting dizzy. When they put me on the chopper I was just going in and out. I can't remember the situation, but I think I walked into the hospital … they had gurneys bringing in so many people. There must have been ten wounded on the chopper. It was a grizzly mess. So, we went into the hospital and they just took two scissors and cut everything off … from my sleeves to my boots. In less than a minute I was just lying there naked. They did some surgery then, and then later I went to Cameron Bay and I was there for a month and a half.

Capt. Hall was calm and in control…I had absolute confidence in him.

Additional Comment: We called the mortar tube High Angle Hell.

Rafael Rivera-Diaz
"PR"

Suddenly hell broke loose.
We had fire coming from everywhere. We got pinned down by an ambush... I recall that Lt. Alvarado had been going forward to help the point man and make sure that he was not in trouble.
So, we start shooting, and they are shooting at us, I remember bullets flying everywhere — I'll always remember that.

Rafael Rivera-Diaz

Nickname: PR - because I came from Puerto Rico
First Platoon

I remember when I arrived in Charlie Company, I was taken to LZ Professional – that's where the company was. They had just come back from an operation where they captured 52 weapons. The first person I met there when I got off the helicopter was Captain Hall. He was the company commander for our company at that time. He called the platoon leader, which was Lt. Alvarado from El Paso, Texas. I remember we called him Diablo because his face looked like a devil. He was a very good platoon leader. So, I was introduced to the platoon. We stayed at LZ Professional until March. That was the time we went to Chop Vum.

We got in there – I remember clear because it was my first mission. We got into a helicopter and were going to a "hot LZ" because they were shooting at us. We came in on a helicopter, I remember the gunner touched me on the shoulder and he said, "When I touch you here, you get out of the plane, because we're getting shot at." At that time another group of people had already arrived. We were the second group, and they were securing the area and were still receiving fire. I remember when that guy touched me on the shoulder and said, "JUMP!" I look and we were high – I mean, we were really high. We could see the rice paddies now, and we just jumped. But we got there, and I remember getting into water up to my chest. I started walking out and the guy behind me grabbed me by my shoulders because he couldn't get out of the rice paddy and he pulled me completely down. So, I was very upset because of that. Meanwhile, we kept moving and we were still receiving fire.

My platoon was the first platoon in Charlie Company, and we were taking the lead that day. I remember so clear, we finally cut through the jungle – it was very heavy – and we started moving. We started moving through the trail. Suddenly hell broke loose. We had fire coming from everywhere. We got pinned down by an ambush. We walked into an ambush. I recall that Lt. Alvarado had been going forward to help the point man and make sure that he was not in trouble. So, we start shooting, and they are shooting at us, I remember bullets flying everywhere – I'll always remember that. And like I was trained – we just put fire on them so we can break contact. We finally got to break fire. I remember killing one person and capturing one.

We started looking at the people we had – and Lt. Alvarado – I remember, he was shot through the head. We had to secure the area until the company went around, and we put everybody in ponchos because we couldn't get them out. I remember Captain Hall specifically. He would be pulling the platoon and people said, "Go check the ponchos, go see if they are alive." And we started unwrapping the ponchos – that's when I could see how Alvarado died (hit in the head). Finally, Captain Hall called and said, "I don't want anybody to be looking at them." So, we closed them back up.

I remember it was late that evening and we couldn't get out, we couldn't move, so we had to spend the night in the area – after we secured the area. So, we had to spend the night with the dead bodies because we couldn't get out and we couldn't get the helicopters in.

I recall the next day they took one other platoon, I think it was third platoon, and they went out to secure some area to see if we could get helicopters in and they got shot at.

One of the guys that got shot had the last name Perez. He was from my home town. I recall at the beginning he didn't know he was shot in the side. He started saying that he was going to die. We couldn't get him out and he was going to die. The medical person called me and said, "I want you to stay with him." I said, "Why?" "Because he wants you to pray for him." So, I started praying for him and I said, "You know you're going to make it."

Finally, that day we tried to move the dead bodies and the wounded to a clearing which was close to a rice paddy. I carried Perez with me, and took him down there to get closer to where the helicopter was coming in. At the same time the helicopter was coming in with some food, which was C-rations. I remember clear that as soon as the helicopters got to the rice paddies, they started receiving fire from three snipers at the same time. So, they threw the C-rations out and took off – they didn't stay. So, we couldn't put the wounded and dead bodies in there. When I am looking at the war movies, I recalled how the bullets ricochet off the ground. I always thought that was a trick from the movies. But I remember at one point when I was trying to get Perez to the helicopter we got shot at and I covered his body, right behind me the ground lifted up three times. I said, "Wow. I guess that's for real."

Perez didn't move. He was shaking. The guy next to me said, "Hey! That guys dead."

I said "No, he's not. He's not dead." I panicked a little bit, and said to Perez, "No, you're not dead." So, finally I lifted up his head, and his eyes opened wide and shook his head and said he's okay. So, finally I got him moved back.

In the meantime, there was a lot of fire coming in. I remember they moved the 90mm, which is like a bazooka, to see if they can knock down the sniper. They couldn't do it, so we had to move back to the area where we started where we had the ambush. Back with the dead bodies and the wounded. We moved from there, not too far, to set up for the night again. So, we spent another night with the dead bodies and the wounded.

The next day we came back where the ambush was, and they took one platoon and they cleared one area and secured it. The helicopters came in and lowered the stretchers to put on the wounded and the dead. They had to put on the dead first because the wounded is more important, because when they get to the hospital, they have to get the wounded off first. So, they went down and got everybody out.

After that we decided we had to get moving because we're still supposed to go help Alpha Company.

So, we move in with ninety-some people in that mission to help Alpha Company. One area we moved to we secured the area, and then we were supposed go up on this hill. We started to go up the hill. As soon as we got up the hill, we hear the pop of the mortar rounds coming in. When we got up that hill there was a big crater – like a bomb crater there. And I was going to jump in there. And one guy grabbed me and said, "No – let's go in this smaller ditch." So, we went in the ditch, and I'm glad we did because the people that jumped in that crater… that's where the mortar rounds went in. I recall three or four or five mortar rounds, I don't know exactly how many. I think when everything cooled, they told us to pull back. And when we pulled back, people started looking in the hole.

Captain Hall said, "Get out of there! Let's move back."

People were in pieces. We had some people cut in pieces. So finally, we took the dead bodies and wounded and moved back. We moved back to where we were during the night. That's one thing I recall is that we had a guy named McCoy, he was the gunner, and that guy, he never wanted to make the fox holes to protect us. He would never do that. I remember he dug one that night so deep that he got himself, another guy, and all their rucksacks and everything in there. One guy said, "You could put another person in there!" He said, "Ya, I don't want to die." So, after that he started digging holes.

After that we took the dead bodies and they started pulling us out of there. We went in with about ninety people and we came out with twenty-seven people. Alpha Company couldn't survive very well. I guess they came out with nineteen people on that mission.

Peggy: "Did you ever find out what happened with Perez?" Yes. People told me who saw him in the hospital said that Perez said, "You helped him, you prayed for him. He made it because of you." He got to New York and he sent me a letter, and he told his family.

Kristin: "What did you do with the guy you captured?" We gave him to the interrogation team. They had to keep him away from everybody. They had to keep him away from us because people wanted to kill him. They took him and put him to headquarters. The helicopter they called was with the CPs, and they interrogate and get him out of there.

Philip Krause

...there were some people that were wounded at that time. There was fighting going on all the while and then darkness came right away. The enemy can lurk better at nighttime than during the day, so you take extra caution. But the thing that bothered me the most was the moaning and groaning of the people that were wounded. All night long this kept up and it was a terrifying thing.

Philip Krause
Third Platoon

We started out sometime in the afternoon (maybe 2:00). We left the LZ and went to the hot LZ, where the enemy was around us and everything. I remember being CA'd in (Combat Assault) and the helicopters would not land on the ground because it was a hot LZ, so we had to jump out and some were pushed out because we were getting shot at.

I jumped out about six feet above the rice paddy. So, I jumped out and carrying all this weight on your back and you jumped into the rice paddies and mud. You sink in and you have to pull yourself back out. After jumping out you finally get out and get going. Then you get to the wood line where everybody else is and start fighting. Then the next group comes in and you protect them as they're getting out of the choppers.

Our rucksack weighed 50 to 60 pounds, plus ammunition strapped to our waist. So, we jumped out, landed in the paddies and got ourselves out. There were some people that were wounded at that time. There was fighting going on all the while and then darkness came right away, and the enemy can lurk better at nighttime than during the day, so you take extra caution. But the thing that bothered me the most was the moaning and groaning of the people that were wounded. All night long this kept up and it was a terrifying thing.

After listening to all that moaning all night, we eventually moved on, but we didn't get too far – maybe 100 meters one way or another because we were just trapped. We couldn't move. We were running low on water, food, ammunition, but what could we do? We moved enough to get ourselves up to a hill and there we sat with some wounded people.

During that same time, we had a short guy out there … he only had about a week before he was to go home, but he wanted to come out and fight with us. Jerry Walls (Muff). Here he was, a guy who was going home in a week, yet he wanted to fight with us. Anyway, they did get some choppers in with more ammunition and water and we sent him out and he jumped on the chopper and made it out of there safely.

We went to a different area and we went from our fox hole to a more open area to get to the helicopters.

When the three stooges went to get water … things looked quiet. "Let's try it!" We had been without water for a long, long time. At least a day or two and it was about 100 degrees. We were sucking on stone pebbles. What do you do … die of thirst? I don't know where we got the water jugs from. Rice paddy water wasn't the greatest water to drink but we had iodine pills to put in it to kill the bacteria. Miller was first, I was second and Feder and Works were behind. Eventually we got Works out.

The sniper let us get out there, spread out, get the water and then he started firing at us. We managed to get back and got in trouble with the Captain.

Additional Comments:

I remember carrying the dead. There were two of us carrying a body in a poncho – one on each end. I had the head end. We came to a wall and we handed the body over feet first. As the guy on the top of the wall pulled, I pushed. An arm fell out of the poncho through the opening. It hung right in front of me. I remember seeing the darkened skin with the gold wedding band.

I believe I was off to the side of the hill. When I heard the first mortar, I went in a trench. I was sitting in the trench counting the mortars coming out of the tube – listening for each one to hit, and wondering if this one would land directly on me. When I heard the explosion from each mortar, I knew I was safe.

Harvy Miller

...all I remember was the water going by and the water bugs in the water. At first, I was trying to miss them but then we decided the iodine pills would take care of them and we just filled them up. We filled up every one of them. It seemed like forever, but it wasn't more than fifteen minutes or twenty minutes. Whoever was next to me, we turned around and started back up the hill, I think it was the sergeant, and the next thing we knew there was rapid AK fire coming from across the creek.

Harvy Miller
Third Platoon

We had been without water for a number of days. I remember one guy that stole some of my bamboo [that had water in it,] and I kept thinking I'm going to shoot him. I don't remember his name. We had gotten to the point of where we were willing to do anything for water.

So, there were four of us – Krause, Feder, me, and Sgt. Barry – we all decided we'd go down because we could see the creek and could hear the water running. There had been some sniper fire from that side, but we thought it was worth the chance to go and get some [water].

So, we gathered all the canteens. As I remember there was like two or three big canteens and then all these little bitty ones. So, we went down to the river and I know I was filling the canteens. There was someone else next to me filling canteens. And all I remember was the water going by and the water bugs in the water. At first, I was trying to miss them but then we decided the iodine pills would take care of them and we just filled them up. We filled up every one of them. It seemed like forever, but it wasn't more the fifteen minutes or twenty minutes.

Whoever was next to me, we turned around and started back up the hill, I think it was the sergeant, and the next thing we knew there was rapid AK fire coming from across the creek. And so the sergeant, who was next to me, he fell on the ground and for some reason this huge rock happened to be there and there were four guys took cover behind the rock. And so, ah, we could hear the AK rounds hitting the backside of the rock. So the sergeant, when he pulled his pant leg up, the round had gone in one side of his knee and on the other side. There was a hole about that big [indicating about two inches] and a big chunk of meat was hanging off. So, I took my Charlie Scarf off and I wrapped it around it and tied it.

By this time, the other members of the unit had started firing everything they had into the other side of the jungle and we ran back as fast as we could. I don't know how many canteens we even got back, probably not very many.

Then we moved from there to the hill that afternoon and that's when they mortared us, and all those people were wounded and killed. And they picked them up and we pulled back to the same place we went down to get the water. That's when the Second Lieutenant we had ... he wasn't there for more than a week, and he got wounded and we were carrying him in a bag.

We were trying to make progress to help Company A. Company A was pinned down and C got pinned down in the process of going to help them. Then when Company C was able to get unpinned, company A had already been picked up.

All I can remember from coming off the hill is carrying that Second Lieutenant. There were four people carrying him in the poncho. We came back to where we got the water and I saw about 50 yards away, an NVA stepped out of the tree line with an RPG and aimed right at them and shot and we all went down and he hit the banana tree right behind us and blew it off the top. He only had one round and headed back into the jungle.

Additional comments:

We were cutting bamboo at the joints, and put the water from it in canteens. We said. "Let's go to the creek." We didn't tell anyone, so we ran the risk of our own people firing at us. I think we took about fifteen canteens and some 1-1/2 quart bladders. I took a big drink, then placed canteens deep enough to fill them.

Three of the men who went to get the water.
Left to right: Philip Krause, Harvy Miller, and Phil Feder

Phillip Feder
"Flip"

The one guy who was with us took a round right through the knee. I had a camera in my pocket, and I took a round right through that camera, which was close enough for me. We were pinned down behind this rock with the M60 machine gun that was shooting one round at a time and you'd have to re-cock it, shoot one shot and re-cock it, and shoot one shot and re-cock.

Phillip Feder
Third Platoon

My nickname was "Flip" – I was one of the very few lucky ones that didn't get wounded.

One of the battles I can talk about is Chop Vum: That was March of 1969. We went into the field with our company of 104 guys, and after six days of heavy fighting we can out with twenty-seven guys. They weren't all killed, there was a lot of wounded. Out of those twenty-seven, ten were wounded. So, we were down in numbers greatly. I just found out tonight at this reunion that our company and A company was up against 8,000 Vietnamese ... it's a time in my life I'll just never forget.

We were all sucking on stones to get some saliva in our mouth. Then finally four of us guys [Flip, Harvy, Phil and one other] went down into the rice paddy with a gallon jug to try and get some water. And we did. We got the jug filled up and we got it up back by some rocks and a sniper opened up on us from the hillside someplace.

The one guy who was with us took a round right through the knee. I had a camera in my pocket, and I took a round right through that camera, which was close enough for me. We were pinned down behind this rock with the M60 machine gun that was shooting one round at a time and you'd have to re-cock it, shoot one shot and re-cock it, and shoot one shot and re-cock.

I know some of the other guys were laying down fire, I'm sure, whenever the sniper was shooting at us. I don't really know where. Someplace along the whole hillside.

Then finally, the company heard that we were pinned down out there. Then they got our position and called it in on the radio and they shot artillery rounds. First, they shoot a smoke round to see our location and be sure it was real close to us in the general vicinity of the enemy and it was ok. Then they opened up with the main rounds and bombarded the whole hillside and we took off dragging Sgt. Barry Works with us. Harvy used his Charlie scarf and wrapped it around Sgt. Barry's knee to try to keep it from bleeding.

Additional Comments:

There were choppers approaching bringing re-supply of ammunition and food. As they drew near, my buddies and I grabbed corners of the poncho which held one of our dead and ran to meet the chopper. As it was about to land, we started taking enemy fire and the chopper couldn't touch all the way down. We attempted to throw our friend into the chopper, but he fell out of the poncho. I grabbed an arm to try and throw him again, but his skin just peeled off of his bone due to the heat and humidity and carrying him in the plastic poncho. I grabbed for him again and this time we got him on. We managed to get everyone out and get some supplies but no water. My hands were covered in rotting flesh, so I had to use a quart of the precious water to clean them.

The last day.

It was a bad situation to be in considering each time the choppers would carry a group out, which meant there were fewer men left to fight off the enemy if the occasion should arise.

The first lift left and took twenty minutes to make it back to us. Seeing how I was part of the last group to get picked up, which meant another twenty minutes I would have to wait. Those were very long twenty-minute stretches and I did a lot of praying during them. When I heard and saw those two beautiful choppers in the sky coming back for us, I had such an exuberant feeling of relief.

John Stringer
"Stringer"

...when we get to Chop Vum, we are kicked out of the chopper at about ten feet off the ground. We land and we have a 30-caliber zeroed in on us. They're up in our face as we land. It's a hot LZ. I remember me and Wilmoth had no place to go. We just moved forward...

John Stringer

Nickname: "Stringer"
Mortar Platoon

You'll see photos with me on the edge of the chopper with my legs kicking and next to me is Wilmoth on the right side and when we get to Chop Vum, we are kicked out of the chopper at about ten feet off the ground. We land and we have a 30-caliber zeroed in on us. They're up in our face as we land. It's a hot LZ. I remember me and Wilmoth had no place to go. We just moved forward; we were trying to knock out a machine gun. We were going right into the fire. It was coming from everywhere. I think we had gotten put into a battalion, as I understand it. But we didn't know that then, we just knew that when we landed, it was a hot LZ and we had nothing to do but go.

Wilmoth had a ninety recoilless. And he was moving forward and there was an E6 from Little Rock next to us, don't remember his name, but I remember as we were trying to go forward I saw his hand coming up and a hand grenade coming up from behind and … and that was our entrance to Chop Vum. You just keep going and don't think about it. You have to forget it.

The E6 jumped up to grab the grenade and it turned out to be a dud, but we didn't know that. He got killed two days later.

The rest of it is just a continuation of the first day.

A lot of the time we didn't know what our goal was, we were just told to do this or that and we did it. Sometimes we had no idea what we were doing or why we were doing it, but it was part of survival.

We had the ninety recoilless; that's what I was carrying then. Dean or Vinny was carrying the mortar. We were the heavy weapons platoon, so we carried the ninety recoilless and the mortars. We usually set them up at night – it depended if we were going to be there for any period of time. It didn't take long to set them up, maybe ten minutes. I think we had a good mortar platoon. Dean was an excellent guy. We had to be fast and accurate.

We learned this later … our main goal was to go in and help Alpha Co. I think that when they put us in, they didn't know that they were including us in a battalion. It was pretty quick. We were having our shit kicked.

I remember me and Wilmoth got separated from the rest of our squad … I don't really know how it happened; I just know we were trying to get across a rice paddy, and we were laying in the NVA perimeter. We were inside the perimeter and our guys were outside the perimeter. I remember we knew an air strike was coming in. I don't know if it was made with napalm … it was these aluminum canister tubes, and we said. "when the napalm leaves the plane, they're going to start getting down and we're going to jump up and run." But the plane came in and we jumped up and the plane dropped high explosives instead of napalm. We turned around and went right back to where we came from. We got out, but I don't know how.

I remember we had finally got our positions dug in and there was a bunker out in front of us. We would get a rocket attack every once in a while and we'd have a big borough in front of us. You couldn't get it in to us, we were dug in pretty good. We'd call in Air Force … they would come right over our holes and we would look up and out of our holes and see the pilots eyes, they were that close and the enemy fire. We would get the shrapnel from the bombs they would throw. They were real long and wide and they would hit into our foxholes. If you stood up, they'd cut your neck off.

We got the order to move out and Dean always carried his shovel and we ended up by a B-52 hole. I put my rucksack down and handed him the shovel because I was carrying it for him. He said, "You're not going to need this," referring to the B-52 hole that all he had to do was set the gun down and about that time the first mortar would be going. My squad – me and Smoke Bringer, and Wilmoth – we jumped over this sniper hole or something, and the first round hit. I wasn't sure where it hit, and the second round hit my rucksack where I had been standing with the ninety. In fact, that was the last time I ever used a ninety recoilless. The second round hit above the sky. I leaned up against it and thought this was stupid, I'm above the ground and I looked around saw Wilmoth and Fiene and they were kind of all laying in a line. I looked around and thought I saw a slight depression round, it was my imagination probably, but I looked around and got down in a fetal position and I could hear the rounds coming down, probably five to six feet behind me. It scared me. There were snipers coming so I got up and went the other way…
We got hit again I think, I don't really remember.

I said yesterday that I didn't know anybody that got killed, but I remember laying there and I knew that I was going home. I thought I had it made. Borges was walking by, so I told him I need to talk to him. He was a hell of a nice guy. I told him to find Vinny because I wanted to talk to him because I was going home, and I want to talk to Dean. He said Deans busy … he can't come over here. I said, "Go get him because I can't go over there." Finally he just said, "Dean's dead." I lost it. I was on the last chopper going out and I was one of the last ones and I heard them putting the bodies on the chopper and the door gunner told me to grab a hold of the belt so he wouldn't slide out. It was Dean's belt.

From there I went to the hospital and cried like a baby and I woke up the next day and John Richardson was standing over my bed and it was really one of the best things because he helped get me through it.

Mortar Platoon

Dick Hall
"Dickie"

...the helicopters came in and there was a lot of smoke. A couple of helicopters went down – they got hit by arms – so they stayed above the smoke... You couldn't see a whole lot. You could hear them whistling, coming by, and you knew what direction they were coming from. Then, it was follow Gary. I had his radio, so wherever Gary went...

Dick Hall
Nickname: "Dickie"
Third Platoon

That's where I got the nickname – over there I was "Dickie."

I got in the country in February. I carried the M-16. I was just following everybody figuring out what was going on. Gary pulled me aside, around the last week of February or the very beginning of March and made me the RTO. So, I was Gary Franklin's RTO. The first thing I did was to learn how to take the radio and stick it down so it went over your pack so that nobody could see the antenna sticking out and you'd get shot at, because that was a target. I knew how to use one from the training and all that.

What I remember is that we'd had a few little shots fired everyday to all hell breaking loose. It seemed to me like it lasted at least 4 days and nights that I remember were pretty heavy, lot of fighting, I was on the radio trying to communicate – trying to be quiet while communicating. Actually, I didn't get out and do a lot of activity because I was the central point. So, if they needed communication that came, I was there. So, Gary and some of the other guys were going out – there was action going on all around me where I wasn't personally involved.

Later on, there was a lot of stuff I was really involved with, where I carried the machine gun and was squad/platoon leader and all that. But right now, mostly for being I was 18, it wasn't a war movie anymore.

Peggy: "When people got wounded, did you call that in?"

Right. Whatever Gary wanted – either that or he'd call for the radio and I would bring the radio to him, and he may call it in or he may call in for communications. But there was so much activity; a lot of communication wasn't done over the radio. It was done by people, you know, passing notes or hand communication. We weren't standing up a lot or running around unless you had to.

There was a progression of guys: You might be a rifleman, a sniper like Jerry. If you carried a radio, of course, you don't have to walk point. As soon as a machine became available, I gave up the radio.

Peggy: "At Chop Vum, one of the things that stood out for most people was that when they got sent in, they had to jump so far into the rice paddies."

Oh Ya! I felt like it was a 50-foot drop when I jumped in there.

Peggy: "And people were shooting at you?"

Oh ya, the helicopters came in and there was a lot of smoke. A couple of helicopters went down – they got hit by arms – so they stayed above the smoke. Now, some people said they got pushed in, but I jumped in. Jumped in, stayed down, and found something to get behind, and tried to figure out where fire was coming from. You couldn't see a whole lot, so just had to either listen or you could hear them whistling, coming by, and you knew what direction they were coming from. Then, it was follow Gary. I had his radio, so wherever Gary went, I went – unless he told me to stand still.

Peggy: "So you made it to the end of that battle? You were one of the last guys that made it out?"

Yes. That was one of three big battles that I remember.

I remember fires and sitting down and watching for the enemy moving around. With the fires burning in the background, if they were moving, you could see them so you could take some sniper shots or pot shots at things moving around. You wanted to be careful, because the flash of the gun could give your position away. If you weren't sure if you could hit them, but they were getting close, you'd probably take a shot to keep them from throwing a grenade in at you.

Additional Comments:

I arrived in Vietnam on Feb.1, 1969. I turned 18 in Vietnam.

I remember running out of food. Adrenaline was running high, so we were really hungry. When we had any pause, we ate.

In Vietnam there was little sense of time. It seems like all one time. Time disappeared in the field.

I realized, I'm not in Kansas anymore.

Vince Tabor
"Vinny"

There was a lull that seemed to proceed toward the back end of the hill and I had gotten up thinking I was good, walked twenty feet, and bumped into one of our good friends.

A mortar round had landed right on him and split him in half and then one of the mortars started coming back in our direction and I realized that they had been walking them right across the hill and back.

I started yelling, "They have the hill patterned, get off the hill!" And I ran back down the hill right back towards Charlie Company. Not too many people heard me because they were ducked down.

Vince Tabor

Nickname: Vinny
Mortar Platoon

I was with the mortars platoon. One of the biggest operations to take place in Vietnam in 68-69 was Chop Vum. I never knew much about it until I came to the reunion.

We were on the third wave of helicopters to land on a hot LZ. Then the machine gun fire came, and we were coming in. The other platoons were knocking out the machine guns. So the helicopters couldn't land on the hot LZ. We had to jump off into the mud of the rice paddy and continue on. That was more secure. They knocked out a machine gun or two and the weapons platoon was safe. Or so we thought.

Then the order was given to go into the thick underbrush and my recollection of what happened next is that the first platoon lead that. And the lieutenant in charge, and the first three men were picked off by North Vietnamese snipers in the brush. When that happened, everyone was spread out at the LZ and I was with the weapons and pretty close. I was one of the ones who slithered in to the underbrush and pulled out the bodies, down the path to the edge of the woods.

At some point we did work our way in. I don't know which platoon led but it wasn't weapons. We brought the bodies with us into a very thick area that was so forested it looked like night during the day. At that point I think it was recognized that we were semi-surrounded. And we stopped right there. A hundred and some men crammed into a spot that was no bigger than seventy by seventy. Where I was in that area was next to bodies ... and we were pinned there for two days. Even the days were like night. We were sleeping next to bodies wrapped in ponchos.

At some point we were able to call a medivac chopper. It was felt we had a secure spot very near to where we were. This may have been the beginning of the third day. Those choppers couldn't even land so the bodies had to be lifted overhead and thrown in. And in some fashion, there had to be six people carrying these bodies in ponchos and a certain number were there to provide security. And everyone kept yelling for the choppers to get lower because they couldn't lift the bodies any higher. And we were cursing. I was a security person and I turned from guarding to curse at the pilots to get them down lower and we told them that we'd shoot their asses down.

After that episode, we went back to this very dark area where we had been, but some probes were sent out into the brush. We had only been there two days and we already needed more ammunition, C-rations, etc. The probe was sent out in one direction and an NVA trench line was found. At that point, the scouts came back and one of the platoons was given the assignment to set themselves up on the line and assault that trench line. A whole slew of firing went on and everyone else in the platoon set up the perimeter and they were able to knock out the NVA. We don't know what happened, but they disappeared and made it to the edge of the rice paddy to get extra supplies. Somehow supplies were dropped but not close to the edge of the wood line where it was safe, but out quite a ways. On the radio we heard these guys would probably take fire on us when we were trying to get the supplies.

We never did get all the supplies. We took what we could get, and what we felt safe getting and came back. This was probably the third day. We tried to get out of there and on our second try we were able to chop through with our machetes. That was the time we chopped through and spread out and there was a foot path and we sat down in some tall grass and as I sat there I saw two NVA that walked between our guys and up the hill and there was no radio near by, so by the time word would get up they would be long gone. And that's just what I saw…

Later in the day, our point man had stepped up over a rock wall and an NVA had jumped up over a spider hole and shot him down and at almost the same time there was a sniper up the hill and an assault that took place. The weapons platoon took their place back on the rock wall and the assault took place and then everyone reassumed their location and pushed forward. Then another sniper opened up from the hilltop and we were coming up to an opening and the sniper opened up and I took a picture … someone standing up in the tall grass shooting at us. As I was hunkered down, we called in an ARVN and these old WWII planes flew where that sniper had been. I don't remember much after that but maybe later that day or the next we moved into an area where we were supposed to link up with Bravo Company who wasn't there yet.

We set up on the opposite side of a small stream on a slight rise, but prior to that, the lead platoon had found a stolen bunker that had been abandoned. We had to slowly move up on that bunker just in case … but there was no one in it.

At that time, it was midday and noon rolled around. Everybody was hunkered down around trees and there was a stone wall separating the abandoned bunker and the stream. On the other side around that tree line came walking along an NVA, an officer with a pistol. He was easily distinguished by the red scarf he had on him that officers wear. And there was a lot of "hush hush" and "get down" and one of our snipers was up at the rock wall and took out the NVA and kept the pistol as a souvenir, and he was showing it off to everyone at the perimeter. So, we were kind of happy that we were getting back at them. Of course, the odds were kind of off, there were about four dead and quite a few wounded and we only had downed two of them.

The next day Bravo was showing up and we decided that we were going to stay overnight on the higher hill. We went up on that hill and Bravo Company took our old place. We spread out on that hill as we normally do for the mortars. We had a pit that was a circle and I started digging it. We had a normal spade; it was hard to dig but we were down maybe six to eight inches and that was when the enemy starting mortaring. I jumped into that pit we were digging for the mortars and a lot of people jumped in that pit. Because we had been there such a short period of time, a lot of people hadn't started digging their fox holes yet. So, people around the mortar pit started jumping in there so I was covered by quite a few people. But I could hear what was going on. There was a lull that seemed to proceed toward the back end of the hill and I had gotten up thinking I was good, walked twenty feet, and bumped into one of our good friends where a mortar round had landed right on him and split him in half, and then one of the mortars started coming back in our direction and I realized that they had been walking them right across the hill and back. I started yelling, "They have the hill patterned, get off the hill!" And I ran back down the hill right back towards Charlie Company. Not too many people heard me because they were ducked down. I went down and after all was over, we moved everybody off of there. This was the ending of the fifth day, we had so many wounded and killed.

And the night before we were bringing the wounded down the hill and there was this one guy from the Bravo Company. One of the RTOs, I believe from headquarters, had wounded his leg. He was still alive, and they brought him down in a poncho and he was coming to. He rose up and saw his leg and he fell back, went into shock, and died almost immediately. So, the person who I saw going up was one of my best friends. We took up with Bravo Company, and I remember distinctly hearing a lot of sobbing and crying all around, even in our fox hole.

Dean Veale. He was down on the ground and got hit right on, his buttocks was split right open, like somebody just took his legs from each side and just split him wide open. We had gone down below and stayed with Bravo Company. The next day we left with only half the platoon, mortar rounds, and rifles. And we just carried as much as we could that day to another hill separate from that … with just twenty-seven left in that company. We split from Bravo Company because the whole operation was to save Alpha Company. Charlie and Bravo were being sent to try and sweep in that direction, link up, and then attack the NVA and get them off Alpha Company and win the operation. We only had twenty-seven men left and had to leave Bravo and they went to find Alpha. We retreated up the hill and were ordered to stay another night on the hill with twenty-seven men. We made fox holes for a maximum of thirty, and we had to wait the whole night and part of the next morning to be extracted by helicopters. It was the most awful experience knowing that you had to stay awake all night and you might not even make it through the night if they knew there were only twenty-seven of us left. Besides that, when the two helicopters landed, it was a small hill and only two could land at a time and they could only take about eight to ten people at a time. So, we went out of our fox holes in some fashion. I got the short straw and was the last one out of the nine in my fox hole. So, at the very end, there were only nine of us left on that hill. And that was the end of Chop Vum. I do not remember what happened after that to build the team back up to 120 men. It's just a blank.

Additional Comments:

When the choppers finally made it in to pick up the wounded, I said "You fuckin' cowards. Get that chopper down lower!"

On day five a North Vietnamese tried to sneak past holding banana leaves, walking sideways. Someone shot him. They got an officer's pistol. It was during the day, in the open.

When we were out of food. I told Stringer, "I have crackers and cheese that I've been saving. We split the can between us, and maybe Jay. We hid while we were eating it.

I stood and, having realized the enemy intention, started yelling, "Get off the hill, they have it patterned!" Moving roughly twenty feet while yelling in all directions, I nearly stumbled over the body of Dean, our weapons platoon squad leader. He had been killed by a direct hit from a mortar round. His body was split apart as if he had been drawn-and-quartered by the legs. This sight sent me into a shocked state, and I do not remember every detail afterwards. However, I did recall yelling "Get off the hill!" and moving back down the hill towards our previous night position.

The next thing I remember was seeing fellow infantrymen carrying the wounded down the hill using ponchos as stretchers. I moved to help and recall seeing "Greg" Gregson, one of the RTOs, being placed on the ground. He had one of his legs blown off during the attack and someone was saying that he was in shock. I was naturally trying to look away because of the blood and gore. However, I noticed that he awakened and lifted his head. Looking down at his body, he fell back to the ground and died.

The last night we dug in deep. We did not sleep at all that night. We were carrying all the weapons we could. On the last day we went to the hill for extraction.

Robert Monger
"Bob"

All of a sudden you heard: Thump. Thump. Thump. And that's mortar coming in. Everybody turned and started to run back towards where we came from... I was huddled down and looking to my left and the mortar shell... I could have reached out and touched where it blew up with my left hand. I can remember going up in the air and I don't know if I flipped or what, but I landed sitting on my butt. I compressed my backbone and I had severed a nerve in my left arm, and it was hanging. I had a big hole here in my chest.

Robert Monger

Nickname: Bob
Mortar Platoon

The first thing that I remember most vividly was they made me the RTO of the Weapons Platoon. I was scared to death, because radio operators don't last very long.

I remember distinctly that my back pack, including the radio, including the extra battery I had to carry, including my five quarts of water, my twenty-four clips of ammunition, and everything – I think I weighed about 170 pounds at that time – But I had a pack of about eighty pounds, I believe. I couldn't get up. If I sat down with my pack on, I couldn't get up, so I had to have help. I remember that very distinctly.

I remember getting on the helicopter, and I told the people on the helicopter that I could not get up so let me sit on the edge, at the very edge of the door. And I remember when I flew into the LZ the helicopter pilot flared too high, and when he leveled the skids he was not three feet off the water, but much higher. And when they leveled the skid, that was the key for the guy behind me to push me out. So, I went out in, I assume, a bomb crater or shell crater because I went in over my head in water. And the only thing I can remember is, "Oh, my God!"

Of course, it's black. You can't see. I remember just walking and finally got over to the dike and I remember sticking my head up enough that I could see. There were Vietnamese running; it looked like they were on the top of the water. My weapon misfired because it had gotten dirty in the water. My first recollection was: break it down, pull the bolt out. I had a jar of the cosmoline stuff and squirted that in there, put the bolt back in there, slammed it shut, held it up over my head, and fired off all the rounds I could fire off. That was when we first landed.

Then, my recollection is, there was a Second Lieutenant on my right, I was in the middle, and Muff, was on my left. And this Second Lieutenant came in the same time I did – we hadn't been there over a couple weeks. He looked at me and said "Tell everybody to get on line. We're going to assault the hill." Well, there were three 51 caliber machine guns on the hill shooting at us, and I'm going "this doesn't make sense." I was afraid to disobey an order, but I was afraid to do it. I looked at Muff, and Muff said, "What did he say?" I said, "He said everybody on line! We're going to assault the hill." And Muff said, "We're not going anywhere. You don't pay any attention to what he is saying, you stay right here." And Muff went over and said something to him; it wasn't kind, I'm very sure. Anyway, the Lieutenant said, "Anyone who doesn't follow me will be in jail when this is over." And he got shot (the lieutenant). And we carried him in a plastic poncho with us – he was dead – until we could get a helicopter to take him out.

We started out, we were looking for Alpha Company, and somebody said there was supposed to be a hospital buried in the mountain. We were supposed to link up to Alpha Company, because they were pinned down, and try to get them out and we were supposed to find this hospital.

One of my worst memories was ... we bivouacked one night, and they told us to dig fox holes. I was so tired I couldn't dig a fox hole. I dug a trench about four or five inches deep, big enough for me to roll in it. And I went to sleep. The next morning somebody said we had a mortar attack. I didn't know anything about it. I remember then, I believe the guy's name was Dean, we were sitting… I'm not sure. I remember being on the side of a hill. As I remember, Dean said, "There goes a Gook." And he said, "There goes another one." And he moved off to our perimeter, kind of. We were not in a bivouac situation. We were kind of going through the jungle. He moved off and then a firefight erupted. And all I know is that there was a Vietcong nurse killed and Dean got killed. He took shrapnel or a round in the brain.

Then we continued to cut through the jungle, and we'd have a firefight now and then. Then, the next thing that really sticks in my mind was we were kind of on a hill and we had to cross this rice paddy. And there was this dike with a trail on. The first platoon and the second platoon had gone across. I'm sitting there and I'm counting these people that are going across because, in my memory, it was like every third one was getting shot at by a sniper. Being the FDC guy, I was pretty good with numbers. I started calculating how many people were in front of me. So, I made sure that I wasn't going to be number three. When I started to run across the rice paddy, he shot at me anyway. And I'll never forget Muff – he was on the other side. He was laying there laughing his head off and I was livid. I was so mad, and I said, "What are you laughing at?" He said, "You looked like the Roadrunner in the cartoons. Your legs from the knees down looked like wheels." So that's how fast I was running.

They told us we had to cross this hill because there was a rice paddy and we didn't want to get bogged down in the rice paddy. As well as I remember, there was some other feature – because the hill was all open. Basically, it didn't have a lot of other vegetation other than grass and stuff. And whatever this other reason was, they didn't want to go the other way. So, they said that we were going to try to go over the hill. Of course, I had my rucksack on and we were trudging up the hill. There was ninety-four of us, if I remember right, that went up. All of a sudden you heard: Thump. Thump. Thump. And that's mortar coming in. Everybody turned and started to run back towards where we came from. And it's like – I don't want to say a cliff, but the ground came down and it dropped off maybe eight, ten feet or so.

There was kind of like a ledge there. Well, I jumped over and crawled up underneath the ledge, trying to dig a hole. And, as well as I remember, I was huddled down and looking to my left and the mortar shell … and I could have reached out and touched where it blew up with my left hand. I can remember going up in the air and I don't know if I flipped or what, but I landed sitting on my butt. I compressed my backbone and I had severed a nerve in my left arm, and it was hanging. I had a big hole here in my chest. And Wilmoth, I think is the guy that came and got me and dragged me over to a bomb crater. And he said, "Get in here and you'll be safe." And I don't know whether he stayed or left. I don't know.

The next thing I remember is they loaded us on a helicopter, and due to the fact that I was walking, they took my arms – my left arm wasn't working – they took and put my arms and crossed them around a post on the helicopter and taped them so I wouldn't fall out. And I was sitting there and I could hear the bullets plink, plink, plink on the side of the helicopter. And the Vietnamese shot an RPG through the helicopter. Both doors were open and I'm sitting there and I saw it come, and it went right through the helicopter. And the pilot just sat there like he was sitting in his chair at home. The next thing, when everybody was loaded, the medic reached up tapped him behind the head twice, and he just eased on out of there. You could hear the bullets: plink, plink, plink, plink.

When I got to the hospital – of course, everybody is worse than me supposedly, so they hauled all them off on gurneys. Somebody come over and cut my bandages and lifted up my left arm and I had a sucking chest wound because my lung had collapsed. So they started screaming, "Get him on a gurney! Get him on a gurney!" So, they took me in and for some reason – I think it was blood loss – they wouldn't put me to sleep. Whatever they gave me, I was higher than a Georgia Pine. I just remember it was surreal – like people were moving around and you could hear them and see their shapes, but I wasn't really there. And I remember that every time he took a piece of shrapnel out he hit the forceps on a piece of – it sounded like porcelain. And I remember one of the thoughts that went through my mind was "she loves me, she loves me not."

I was at the 27th Surg for two weeks. I had a chest tube, and I carried a one-gallon jug like you carry kerosene in for a long time. The worst pain I had out of the whole situation was when they pulled the chest tube out. Then I went to Cameron for two weeks. Then I went to Camp Drake, in Tokyo for about a month. Then I went to Walter Reed. From there I went to Fort Meade in Maryland and I stayed there a couple of months and then I got out.

I was basically in country maybe eight to ten weeks and I have never been around a group of guys that I think about daily. I think about them daily.

Henry Long
"Carrot Top"

We had fire coming from the front of us. I think
that's what everybody was concentrating on – trying
to find out the location and lay down fire in front of
them.
In the meantime, I thought I heard automatic
weapons fire from in back of us. I think they were
being picked on by the weapons fire behind us, and
the other guys were keeping the other bad guys
down. But if that's true or not,
I don't know. I just know we lost some people out
there.

Henry Long

Nickname: Carrot Top or Long
First Platoon

They called me Carrot Top when I was an RTO and I had red hair. But other than that, everyone called me Long.

As far as Chop Vum goes, I remember being at LZ Professional. We were up there for about a week on the hill, and then we'd usually go out to the field. We got down to the helicopter pad to go out into the field, and then we heard our orders were changed. We had to go out and help Alpha Company because they were pinned down somewhere. So, as things went along, we all jumped onto the helicopters and went out to a rice paddy-type hot LZ. We jumped out of the helicopters. Some got into some muddy-type hard terrain. I don't remember it being that muddy, it was muddy enough that you had to trudge to the edge of the paddy.

I was in the first platoon, so I was on the first load out. Then we made our way to the side of the rice paddy, the landing zone. Then we kinda held position until some more choppers arrived.

Then we were told to go on in. Our platoon took off first because we were there first. So that's when Lieutenant Alvarado and our platoon started heading into the wood line. Then we got through some heavy cover and walked into a small opening. I didn't see nothing. Apparently, I was about seven or eight people back from the front. Lieutenant Alvarado started walking across that opening and that's when they opened up. We had fire coming from the front of us. I think that's what everybody was concentrating on – trying to find out the location and lay down fire in front of them.

In the meantime, I thought I heard automatic weapons fire from in back of us. I think they were being picked on by the weapons fire behind us, and the other guys were keeping the other bad guys down. But if that's true or not, I don't know. I just know we lost some people out there. We lost two right away, and one died early the next morning because we couldn't get him medevaced out. It was right at dusk, and the choppers were taking a lot of hits. It's the first time I remember us not getting people out of there who were hit. I don't think it ever happened again in my memory.

My memories of Chop Vum were very sporadic. I remember three primary days. The day we went in and the day we went farther up the hill into open area, and we took some mortar rounds. I jumped into a big crater, along with the radio operators – the Captain's operators. I was the only one that walked out of the hole that I know of. I walked over to the edge of the hilltop and got into a trench line where we were able to pick up smoke from the mortar rounds that were coming in to us. We started laying down fire and the mortar rounds stopped. Whether we hit anything we don't know. But we certainly know that they stopped firing. That was very traumatic with people were being lost the day before. It seemed like the next day, but I don't know exactly.

The other day I remember is after we'd been around there for a while. We'd been pinned down and everything else. The day we got out of there. We turned and went the opposite direction of what everybody thought we were going. So did Alpha Company – the company we were trying to help. We all walked out of there. We thought sure we were going to get into something bad. But we walked out of there without a casualty. Out helicopters got out. It just amazed me that we got out of there alive – not a one of us thought that we would.

I know it was more than three days, but that's what I remember.

Gary Franklin
"Frank"

The mortars were coming off pretty good. We started off down the hill but didn't make it. And there was a foxhole and I was lighter and quicker than Flip [Phil Feder], and Flip was dragging the gun. So, I beat him to the foxhole, and I jumped in and in comes somebody else and jumped on top and it was Flip. He landed right on top of me and then somebody jumped on top of Flip. They were yelling "Get down!" and I was yelling "Get off!" because I landed on my hands and knees, and I looked down and there was a Bouncing Betty dead center of that foxhole. And here I had two guys on top of me, and I knew that if my arms gave out, we'd come down on that Bouncing Betty we'd come out fast...

Gary Franklin

Nickname: Frank
Third Platoon

The second platoon was the first in and they were put at point. And they called us back and said that one of the door gunners was pushing people out. They were pushing people out 8 or 10 feet up. Collins and I were in there and Collins unlatched the door gunner's strap and put his 14 [M14 rifle] on his head and said, "You're gonna be the first one out, I don't think you better push people."

The door gunner turned around and looked at Collins and down the barrel of the M14 and took his hand back and he didn't push anybody else out that door. We put a stop to that. He was pushing people out at ten to fifteen feet up.

This was right after the big mortar attack. We lost everybody. Fiene and Sheffield got hurt and most of the guys made it to the base of the hill, but Collins and I went to get the wounded. We forgot that both of us could carry one guy faster than each of us carrying one. So I had him by the legs and Collins had him by the shoulders and we were coming down the hill with him and they shot an RPG across the rice patties after the others were out there getting water and I saw him come about halfway out of there [the jungle] and hit a banana tree about 10 feet from us and blew the banana tree about all the way into the rice patty, and Collins gave him a piece of his mind. He said "that's the best you so-and-so's can do? You can't even hit nothing…" and I said, "good…Egg 'em on Jerry! Maybe they'll do better next time."

We put the guy we were carrying down behind the rock fence for a bit and Jerry was dying to get down there. And then I found out the reason he was dying to get down there was that he saw the original "pop." So, he knew where the RPG came from. So, we put the guy behind the rock fence and I told him don't go anywhere we'd be right back … but he wasn't gonna go nowhere. He was hurting quite bad. We ran down there and helped the others shoot across the rice patty a couple rounds and then we ran back up there and he was still there waiting for us. And I'll bet he thought "I hope you people are better than the last heroes that got me who brought me down the hill and dropped me."

So, then we went back and got him. And that was really the only time I got close to getting shot at from an RPG.

The mortars were coming off pretty good. We started off down the hill but didn't make it. And there was a foxhole and I was lighter and quicker than Flip [Phil Feder], and Flip was dragging the gun. So, I beat him to the foxhole, and I jumped in and in comes somebody else and jumped on top and it was Flip. He landed right on top of me and then somebody jumped on top of Flip. They were yelling "Get down!" and I was yelling "Get off!" because I landed on my hands and knees, and I looked down and there was a Bouncing Betty dead center of that foxhole. And here I had two guys on top of me. My first thought was this is better than a sandbag bunker; I can take a direct hit before it hurts me. And I knew that if my arms gave out, we'd come down on that Bouncing Betty we'd come out fast. And I was yelling, "Get out!" and Flip was yelling "Get down!." I guess he finally heard me yelling get out and they piled off me and boy, we got out of there and we took off by the others and ran right off that cliff. We didn't even look to see how far it was. We just ran right straight off it as fast and hard as we could. It could have been 100 feet or 10 feet, didn't matter, we just ran straight off it. It only was about 8-10 feet. Most of the third platoon got off there real fast. Most of the third platoon were the only ones that survived. We were off the hill by the time the first mortar round hit.

We talked to that photographer that was with us. He was digging foxholes every few minutes. We told him we'd only be there about 10 minutes, but he didn't care. We talked to him about going to Chop Vum and he was all excited.

He said he heard it was gonna be great fighting and I asked, "Did you have to go, or did you volunteer to come do this?"

He said, "I volunteered!"

I said, "Get on that chopper and get out of here."

"It's gonna be great!"

"No…it ain't gonna be great."

His excitement wore off about halfway off of that hot LZ. His excitement was gone. And once he was there, he couldn't go back. Only the badly wounded went out and then the dust offs were getting shot down so no one wanted to go anywhere. He did want to get on every chopper, but couldn't.

They were bringing in ammunition and taking out the badly wounded. They weren't taking any bodies; they weren't bringing in any food or water. Only ammunition in and badly wounded out. They were getting shot at so much they didn't want to carry any extra weight. They were coming in as fast as they could.

Additional Comments:

The temperature was probably 110 degrees during the day.

The first night I sat up close to the first platoon. I looked for a low area in the crater to hold up Koehn. I was holding Koehn up so he could breath. The medic and I took turns holding him during the night so he could stay sitting up. My shirt was completely soaked with Koehn's blood.

First extractions out of Chop Vum they brought ammunition. They took out the wounded, not walking wounded or dead.

I was out of water for a day and a half. Everyone was told not to go to get water. There was a rice paddy from years before. A stream ran into it. When they ran across the rice paddy earlier – everyone had seen it – they were forbidden to stop. When we saw the guys getting water, we couldn't believe it. Sheffeld said, You stupid F*****s.

We put out everything we could into the perimeter to protect them after sniper fire started. When they got back with the water there were holes in the jug. Sheffield chewed the guys out.

One of the medics had a breakdown. He cried and rocked all night long after the weapons attack.

Jerry Collins
Third Platoon

They told me I was going on a vacation to a tropical paradise with beautiful girls and swaying palm trees. They didn't tell me the girls were going to be in the palm trees shooting at me. At that point everything just kind of deteriorated.

HISTORY OF THE CHARIE SCARF

The scarf came from a village next to Chu Lai. It was just north of the 18th Brigade. Everybody used to sneak out and buy gum, and the supply sergeant had a girlfriend who was a seamstress. So, he commissioned her to make these scarves. I don't know where the red "C" came from. It's all cotton — the same thing they made their pajamas from. We made them for a morale booster. Charlie Company was always in fights and we didn't abuse the bad guys, which is a good thing. If you're always getting hurt but not getting to shoot at them you get a little bit ornery.

But one day, the point man got shot. By the time I got there they had propped this Vietnamese soldier up and there was a cigarette burning in his mouth. It was kind of funny at the time, but then I thought that may be a precursor of them doing something worse. So, I thought let's get some scarves and basically you kill the guy and put them over his head like a shroud. We left a bunch of them there. As a matter of fact, we went in and wiped out almost a whole company in an ambush. And when we caught a couple of them the next day, they said there was a bounty for our company because we left the scarves.

The scarves started at LZ Professional in 1969. The girl made about a hundred of them and I wasn't sure if people would like them, so the deal was that they should either wear it around their neck, keep it in their pocket to clean their weapon with, or keep it to use as a handkerchief. But if somebody comes up and says show me your scarf, you better have one. I don't think it was very long until everybody was really proud of them.

Jamie Hall

Philip Krause and Phil Feder wearing their Charlie Scarfs

This is a Memorial Tribute to the men of Charlie Company, 1/52nd, 198th Light Infantry Brigade, Americal Division, who served with exceptional courage and fortitude.
These men gave all at Chop Vum.

Raul Alvarado, Jr

First Lieutenant
C CO, 1ST BN, 52ND INFANTRY, 198TH INFANTRY BDE
AMERICAL DIV, USARV
Army of the United States
El Paso, Texas
May 29, 1947 to March 03, 1969
RAUL ALVARADO Jr is on the Wall
Panel W30, Line 18

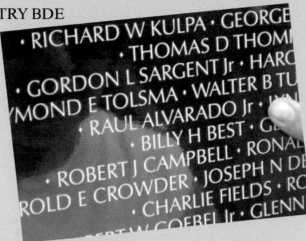

Paul Donald Cooke

Private First Class
C CO, 1ST BN, 52ND INFANTRY, 198TII INFANTRY BDE
AMERICAL DIV, USARV
Army of the United States
La Place, Louisiana
May 28, 1948 to March 03, 1969
PAUL D COOKE is on the Wall
Panel W30, Line 20

Ronald Jay Vanden Berg

Sergeant
C CO, 1ST BN, 52ND INFANTRY, 198TH INFANTRY BDE
AMERICAL DIV, USARV
Army of the United States
Wyoming, Michigan
March 26, 1947 to March 03, 1969
RONALD J VANDENBERG is on the Wall
Panel W30, Line 34

Oliver Kenneth Webb

Private First Class
C CO, 1ST BN, 52ND INFANTRY, 198TH INFANTRY BDE
AMERICAL DIV, USARV
Army of the United States
Valdosta, Georgia
March 31, 1947 to March 03, 1969
OLIVER K WEBB is on the Wall

Panel W30, Line 34

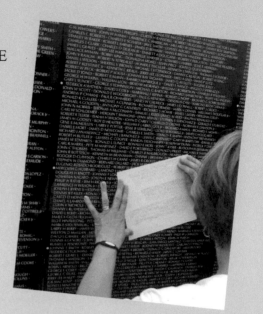

Arlin Wayne Koehn

Specialist Four
C CO, 1ST BN, 52ND INFANTRY, 198TH INFANTRY BDE
AMERICAL DIV, USARV
Army of the United States
Helena, Oklahoma
May 23, 1948 to March 03, 1969
ARLIN W KOEHN is on the Wall
Panel W30, Line 26

David Daniel Layne

Specialist Four
3RD PLT, C CO, 1ST BN, 52ND INFANTRY, 198TH INFANTRY BDE
AMERICAL DIV, USARV
Army of the United States
Chatham, Virginia
January 10, 1950 to March 07, 1969
DAVID D LAYNE is on the Wall
Panel W30, Line 66

Thomas Robert Gregson
Specialist Four
C CO, 1ST BN, 52ND INFANTRY, 198TH INFANTRY BDE
AMERICAL DIV, USARV
Army of the United States
Attica, Michigan
November 27, 1947 to March 08, 1969
THOMAS R GREGSON is on the Wall
Panel W30, Line 75

Kenneth Edward Miller
Specialist Four
C CO, 1ST BN, 52ND INFANTRY, 198TH INFANTRY BDE
AMERICAL DIV, USARV
Army of the United States
New Boston, Michigan
June 01, 1948 to March 08, 1969
KENNETH E MILLER is on the Wall
Panel W30, Line 79

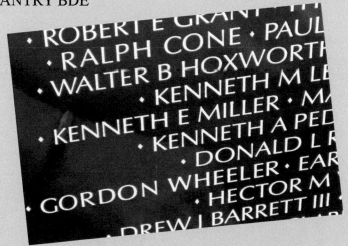

Ralph Dean Veale
Sergeant
C CO, 1ST BN, 52ND INFANTRY, 198TH INFANTRY BDE
AMERICAL DIV, USARV
Army of the United States
King City, Missouri
July 14, 1948 to March 08, 1969
RALPH D VEALE is on the Wall
Panel W30, Line 82

LZ PROFESSIONAL

LZ Professional in background

Helicopter Pad

Men lined up by Helicopter Pad ready to leave for Chop Vum

Philip Krause by Bunker 16

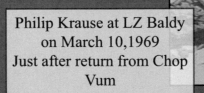

Philip Krause at LZ Baldy on March 10,1969 Just after return from Chop Vum

This book is dedicated to honor the members of the 1/52nd Infantry, 198th LIB, Americal Division.

Each man has his own story. Sometimes the accounts of the same battle are different. This is understandable. Each person was in a different place and saw a different view. These interviews took place an average of forty years after the battle.

It makes no difference to me who is most accurate. The important thing is that each man shared their story.

Notes

These interviews were conducted at a Charlie Company Reunion spanning over many years. They were video recorded and then transcribed. The interviews were conducted by Kristin Hamilton and me.

After the decision was made to write a book to capture the battle at Chop Vum, many questions arose in my mind. At each reunion I asked more questions and the Veterans filled me in on more details. These were recorded in notebooks, and are not direct quotes by the Veterans. However, there were many things they remembered as we talked, and I wanted to include them in this book. Therefore, I have taken the liberty of adding some "Additional Comments" at the end of their transcription.

The novel, *The Men Behind the Scarf,* is the companion work to these Charlie Company interviews. Like this book, it is available on Amazon.com.

Peggy Krause

Made in the USA
Monee, IL
30 October 2021